T2-EVX-232

HOW TO MAKE LIFE EASIER

Commuting to work, driving the kids to soccer, balancing the checkbook—each and every day is so full, who's got time to get wholesome dinners on the table? You will—when you use Del Monte 2 NITE RECIPES™.

WHAT IS THE DEL MONTE 2 NITE RECIPES COOKBOOK?

■ It's a **menu cookbook** that offers a flexible way to plan and organize your dinners.

■ It's a **time-saver** that helps you plan two dinner menus at once.

■ It's a **handy kitchen guide** that offers practical tips on food storage, entertaining and lots more!

Our 2 NITE RECIPES give you a little more time for yourself. Go ahead, play tennis or take up ballroom dancing. You deserve it.

HERE'S WHAT YOU GET

✔ **MORE FREE TIME:** We've organized the recipes, shopping lists and menus so you'll spend less time shopping, cooking and cleaning up.

✔ **VARIETY IN MEALS:** We've included over 60 quick and easy recipes organized into 32 menu plans. In addition, there's a special holiday section full of festive recipes, tips for entertaining and a plan that organizes your cooking.

✔ **FLEXIBILITY:** You design a plan to suit your lifestyle, tastes and schedule. On the *Cook Day*, put together whatever recipe you choose and use the extra amounts of ingredients you cook whenever you please on the *Quick Day*. That *Quick Day* can be the next day or the day after (or freeze the extra ingredients for next month).

✔ **LESS STRESS:** Since we've planned and organized your meals for you, you have one less thing to think about.

HERE'S HOW IT WORKS

1. **Choose a menu set.** A *Cook Day* and its accompanying *Quick Day* or any suitable *Quick Day* you choose.

2. **Shop once for two dinners.** Use both menus' recipe ingredient lists as a shopping list, buying only those items listed in black. All recipes call for common, readily available ingredients.

3. **Follow the simple, step-by-step recipe instructions.**

4. **Cook a complete meal on the *Cook Day*,** cooking extra of some of the ingredients to make an entirely different meal on the *Quick Day*.

5. **Follow the colored arrows** at the bottom of each page to go back and forth between the *Cook Day* and the *Quick Day* recipes, if you need to.

6. **Take it easy on the *Quick Day!***

THE DEL MONTE DIFFERENCE

The Del Monte name goes back more than 100 years to when the Oakland Preserving Company named their premium quality canned goods Del Monte, "from the mountain." Today, consumers know the Del Monte brand stands for premium quality, just as it did 100 years ago. When you buy Del Monte, you're buying the best.

■ At Del Monte, we can most of our fruits and vegetables within 24 hours of harvesting, when flavor and nutrients are at their peak.

■ Del Monte canned fruits and vegetables are on hand and affordable year-round, when seasonal produce may be unavailable.

■ Fruits and vegetables packed under our label meet strict quality standards.

■ The high heat used in the canning process preserves the food just like home canning does, **so we never need to add preservatives**.

■ Our cans are recyclable steel—they're made with 30% recycled steel, the maximum amount that one could use.

■ More than 20 years ago, Del Monte was the first company to use voluntary nutritional labeling and is one of the first to comply with the new 1994 nutritional labeling regulations.

■ Our fruits and vegetables add variety and a balance of nutrients to your diet. These convenient products make it easy to eat your 5-A-Day. Eating 5 or more servings of fruits and vegetables daily is recommended by the National Cancer Institute, the U.S. Department of Health and Human Services, the U.S. Department of Agriculture and the National Academy of Sciences. Our fruits and vegetables make quick and tasty meals, while our convenient, shelf-stable single-serving cups make great on-the-go snacks.

■ Our 2 NITE RECIPES™ were created and tested by professional home economists. Understanding the demands of your hectic lifestyle, they developed these quick, nutritious menus to be flexible enough to fit your family's mood and schedule.

At Del Monte, we are in tune with today's lifestyles and consumer trends, so we offer a line of products that gives you, the consumer, a choice. Our tomatoes are precut and preseasoned, ready to make quick sauces, soups and entrées. Our tomato and vegetable products come in regular or no-salt-added varieties. Our fruits are packed in heavy or light syrup, or in 100% natural juice. We make single serving Snack Cup® products (fruit, pudding and gel cups) that are convenient, ready-to-eat and delicious—and they don't need refrigeration.

COOK DAY

Italian style
stewed tomatoes,
garlic and bacon
make this quick-
to-fix dish rich
and flavorful.
Cook double the
amount of chicken
and rice, and a
second meal is
ready in no time.

DO-AHEAD NOTE

■ Cook extra chicken
and rice.

MEDITERRANEAN CHICKEN

4 slices bacon, diced
8 half boneless chicken breasts, skinned (cook all and save 4 for Quick Day, page 8)
1 can (14½ ozs.) DEL MONTE® Italian Style Stewed Tomatoes

6 medium pitted black olives, cut into quarters (optional)
2 large cloves garlic, minced, *or* ¼ tsp. garlic powder

1. In large skillet, cook bacon over medium-high heat 2 minutes (bacon will not be done); remove bacon from skillet, reserving drippings in skillet.

2. Flatten chicken slightly with palm of hand; season with salt and pepper, if desired. Place 4 chicken breasts in bacon drippings in skillet; cook 6 minutes on each side or until chicken is no longer pink in center. (Cool, cover and refrigerate this cooked chicken for Quick Day, page 8.) Return bacon to skillet. Add remaining 4 chicken breasts; cook 6 minutes on each side or until chicken is no longer pink in center.

3. Add tomatoes, olives and garlic to skillet; cook, uncovered, about 5 minutes or until slightly thickened.   *4 servings*

Prep time: 5 minutes   **Cook time:** 30 minutes

S E R V E   W I T H

CONFETTI RICE

2½ cups uncooked long-grain white rice (cook all and save 3 to 4 cups cooked rice for Quick Day, page 8)
1 can (8½ ozs.) DEL MONTE Peas and Carrots, drained
2 Tbsp. butter or margarine
2 Tbsp. chopped parsley

In medium saucepan, cook rice according to package directions. (Cool, cover and refrigerate 3 to 4 cups cooked rice for Quick Day, page 8.) Stir vegetables, butter and parsley into remaining rice; heat through.   *4 servings*

BREAD STICKS

CHILLED DEL MONTE SLICED PEACHES OVER RASPBERRY SORBET OR STRAWBERRY ICE CREAM

7

Turn page for Quick Day recipe

SWEET AND SPICY CHICKEN STIR-FRY ▣

**1 can (8 ozs.) DEL MONTE®
Pineapple Chunks In Its Own
Juice, undrained**
2 tsp. vegetable oil
**1 large green bell pepper, cut into
strips**
4 half boneless chicken breasts,
skinned, cooked and cut bite-
size (cooked on Cook Day,
page 7)

¾ cup sweet and sour sauce
**⅛ to ½ tsp. crushed red pepper
flakes**
3 to 4 cups cooked rice (cooked on
Cook Day, page 7)

1. Drain pineapple, reserving ⅓ cup juice.

2. In large skillet, heat oil over medium-high heat. Add green pepper; stir-
fry 2 minutes.

3. Add chicken, sweet and sour sauce, crushed red pepper flakes and
pineapple; stir-fry 3 minutes or until heated through.

4. Meanwhile, place rice in microwavable dish; sprinkle with 2 teaspoons
water. Cover with plastic wrap; slit to vent. Microwave on HIGH 4
minutes or until heated through.* Spoon onto serving plate; top with
chicken mixture. Garnish, if desired.   *4 servings*

Prep time: 5 minutes   **Cook time:** 5 minutes

*If microwave is not available, bring ⅓ cup water to a boil in medium
saucepan. Add cooked rice. Reduce heat to low; cover and cook about 10
minutes or until heated through, stirring occasionally. (Rice scorches
easily so avoid high heat.)

S E R V E   W I T H
**TOSSED GREEN SALAD WITH SLICED RED
ONIONS**

Turn
back for
Cook Day
recipes

8

QUICK DAY

There isn't a quicker stir-fry since you cook the chicken and rice ahead, page 7. Use less red pepper for a milder dish or more for a fiery one.

TIP

■ Look for sweet and sour sauce in the international section of the supermarket.

COOK DAY

This chicken is great right off the grill or tasty later in salads, sandwiches or almost any recipe calling for cooked chicken. Grill extra to make Grilled Chicken Taco Salad, page 12.

TIP

■ Start the coals about 40 minutes before you plan to cook.

DO-AHEAD NOTE

■ Grill extra chicken.

HICKORY BBQ CHICKEN

1 can (15 ozs.) DEL MONTE®
Hickory Sloppy Joe Sauce
¼ cup fresh lime juice

8 half boneless chicken breasts,
skinned (cook all and save
4 for Quick Day, page 12)

1. Reserve ½ cup sauce to serve over cooked chicken; cover and refrigerate until 30 minutes before serving. Stir lime juice into remaining sauce in can. Arrange chicken in 11×7-inch dish. Cover with sauce mixture from can; turn to coat. Cover and refrigerate at least 30 minutes or overnight.

2. Grill chicken over hot coals (or broil) 4 minutes per side or until no longer pink in center, brushing chicken occasionally with marinade. (Cool, cover and refrigerate 4 cooked chicken breasts for Quick Day, page 12.) Serve remaining chicken with reserved ½ cup sauce. (Any remaining marinade must be boiled for several minutes before serving with chicken.) *4 servings*

Prep time: 5 minutes **Marinate time:** 30 minutes **Cook time:** 10 minutes

---

S E R V E   W I T H

WARM FRENCH BREAD

MARINATED CORN AND PEPPER SALAD
1 can (11 ozs.) DEL MONTE Summer Crisp
Corn, drained
½ red or green bell pepper, diced
2 green onions, sliced
Oil and vinegar dressing

In medium bowl, combine corn, pepper and onions; toss with dressing. Garnish, if desired. *4 servings*

ICY PEACH SLUSH
1 can (16 ozs.) DEL MONTE Sliced Peaches,
frozen in can

Immerse can in hot water for a few minutes to thaw slightly. Drain fruit, reserving syrup. Pour syrup into blender. Cut fruit into chunks. Add to blender; blend until smooth. *4 servings*

11

Turn
page for
Quick Day
recipes

GRILLED CHICKEN TACO SALAD

1 can (14½ ozs.) DEL MONTE®
    Mexican Style Stewed
    Tomatoes
⅓ cup medium or hot salsa
2 Tbsp. vegetable oil
2 Tbsp. vinegar, such as red wine
    or cider
1 large head romaine lettuce,
    chopped (about 10 to
    12 cups)

4 half boneless chicken breasts,
    grilled and cut bite-size
    (cooked on Cook Day,
    page 11)
1 can (8 ozs.) kidney beans,
    drained (optional)
1 cup (4 ozs.) shredded sharp
    Cheddar cheese
3 cups broken tortilla chips

1. Drain tomatoes, reserving 1 tablespoon liquid. Chop tomatoes; set aside.

2. In small bowl, make dressing by blending reserved tomato liquid, salsa, oil and vinegar.

3. In large bowl, toss lettuce with tomatoes, chicken, beans and cheese. Add dressing as desired. Add chips; toss. Season with salt and pepper, if desired. Serve immediately. Garnish, if desired.

4 main-dish servings

Prep time: 15 minutes

S E R V E   W I T H

HOT BUTTERED TORTILLAS
    Flour or corn tortillas
    Butter or margarine

Wrap desired number of tortillas in plastic wrap. Microwave on HIGH 15 seconds or until warm. Remove plastic wrap; spread with butter. Serve immediately. Or, wrap in foil and heat in conventional oven at 350°F 5 to 7 minutes or until warm.

Turn
back for
Cook Day
recipes

QUICK DAY

Grill extra chicken on the Cook Day, page 11, to add to this salad at the end of a busy day.

Or, if you want something hot, make Beef Steak Chili, page 52, instead, substituting this chicken for the beef.

TIP

■ Try adding avocado, green onions, olives, corn, radishes or cilantro as desired.

COOK DAY

The aroma of the herbed chicken cooking will bring the family in before you have a chance to announce dinner is ready. Cook some extra chicken for the Quick Day, page 16.

DO-AHEAD NOTE

■ Cook extra chicken.

TIP

■ Be sure to buy the groceries for both the Cook and Quick Days.

ROSEMARY CHICKEN AND VEGETABLES

4 carrots, cut into thick julienne strips
3 baking potatoes, cut bite-size
1½ tsp. garlic salt, divided
½ tsp. rosemary leaves, crushed, divided

3 lbs. cut-up chicken, skin trimmed
4 half chicken breasts (cook all for Quick Day, page 16)

1. Preheat oven to 400°F.

2. In 13×9-inch or 3-quart baking dish, combine vegetables with ½ teaspoon garlic salt and ¼ teaspoon rosemary. Arrange *all* of the chicken over vegetables; sprinkle with remaining 1 teaspoon garlic salt and ¼ teaspoon rosemary. Season with salt and pepper, if desired.

3. Bake 30 to 40 minutes or until chicken is no longer pink in center and vegetables are tender. (Cool, cover and refrigerate 4 chicken breasts for Quick Day, page 16.) Garnish, if desired.   *4 to 6 servings*

Prep time: 5 minutes
Bake time: 40 minutes

S E R V E   W I T H

PEAR SPINACH SALAD
4 cups torn spinach leaves
1 can (16 ozs.) DEL MONTE® Lite Sliced Pears, drained
⅓ cup thinly sliced red onions
Italian dressing

In large bowl, toss spinach, pears and onions with enough dressing to coat.   *4 servings*

PEACH MELBA
½ cup seedless raspberry jam
1 can (16 ozs.) DEL MONTE Yellow Cling Peach Halves, drained
1 pt. (16 oz.) vanilla ice cream

In small saucepan, heat jam; set aside. Place peaches in 4 serving dishes. Top with ice cream and warm jam.
4 servings

DINNER ROLLS

15

Turn page for Quick Day recipes

SKILLET RANCH CHICKEN

1 onion, chopped
1 Tbsp. vegetable oil
1 can (14½ ozs.) DEL MONTE® Italian or Original Style Stewed Tomatoes
½ tsp. thyme, crushed

4 half chicken breasts, baked and skinned (baked on Cook Day, page 15)
1 can (15¼ ozs.) DEL MONTE Sweet Peas, drained
1 can (10¾ ozs.) condensed cream of celery soup

1. In large skillet, cook onion in oil over medium heat until tender. Stir in tomatoes and thyme. Cook, stirring occasionally, until thickened; keep warm.

2. Arrange chicken in shallow microwavable dish; cover. Microwave on HIGH 4 to 5 minutes or until heated through.

3. Just before serving, stir peas and soup into skillet; heat through. Add chicken; spoon sauce over chicken.   *4 servings*

Prep & cook time: 16 minutes

S E R V E   W I T H

DILLED CARROT SALAD
¼ tsp. dill weed
1 can (8¼ ozs.) DEL MONTE Sliced Carrots, drained
5 cups torn romaine lettuce
Dijon dressing

In large bowl, sprinkle dill over carrots. Add lettuce; toss with dressing.   *4 servings*

BUTTERMILK BISCUITS

Turn back for Cook Day recipes

QUICK DAY

Already baked chicken, page 15, reheats nicely in this microwave recipe. And dinner's a lot less fussy when the chicken is already cooked!

If you prefer, you may use this chicken instead of tuna to make Tarragon Tuna Pasta Salad, page 40.

COOK DAY

Peanut sauce with chicken is still the rage. When it's not too spicy, it's loved by kids and adults alike. Be sure to cook some extra chicken so you can easily make Mandarin Chicken Salad, page 20, in the next day or so.

DO-AHEAD NOTE

■ Cook extra chicken.

PEANUT CHICKEN

8 half boneless chicken breasts, skinned (cook all and save 4 for Quick Day, page 20)
2 Tbsp. vegetable oil
1 can (14½ ozs.) DEL MONTE® Original Style Stewed Tomatoes, coarsely chopped

2 cloves garlic, minced, *or* ¼ tsp. garlic powder
¼ tsp. ground ginger *or* 1 tsp. grated ginger root
⅛ to ¼ tsp. crushed red pepper flakes
3 Tbsp. peanut butter

1. In large skillet, cook chicken in hot oil over medium-high heat about 4 minutes on each side or until chicken is no longer pink in center. Remove chicken from skillet. (Cool, cover and refrigerate 4 cooked chicken breasts for Quick Day, page 20.)

2. Add tomatoes, garlic, ginger and red pepper to skillet; cook 2 minutes. Stir in peanut butter.

3. Return chicken to skillet; heat through. Sprinkle with chopped cilantro and peanuts, if desired.   *4 servings*

Prep time: 4 minutes
Cook time: 12 minutes

S E R V E   W I T H

GARLIC GREEN BEANS
1 can (14½ ozs.) DEL MONTE Whole Green Beans, drained
2 tsp. butter or margarine
2 cloves garlic, minced, *or* ¼ tsp. garlic powder

In small saucepan, cook green beans with butter and garlic until heated through.
4 servings

PARSLEY RICE

WHOLE WHEAT DINNER ROLLS

19

Turn page for Quick Day recipes

MANDARIN CHICKEN SALAD

1 can (15½ ozs.) DEL MONTE®
   Pineapple Chunks in Heavy
   Syrup, undrained
3 Tbsp. vegetable oil
3 Tbsp. cider vinegar
1 Tbsp. soy sauce
4 cups shredded cabbage or
   lettuce

1 can (14½ ozs.) DEL MONTE
   Diced Tomatoes, drained
4 half boneless chicken breasts,
   skinned, cooked and cut
   bite-size (cooked on Cook
   Day, page 19)
⅓ cup packed cilantro, chopped,
   or ½ cup sliced green onions

1. Drain pineapple, reserving ¼ cup syrup for dressing. In small bowl, combine reserved syrup, oil, vinegar and soy sauce; stir briskly with fork.

2. In large bowl, toss cabbage with pineapple, tomatoes, chicken and cilantro. Add dressing as desired; gently toss.

3. Sprinkle with toasted slivered almonds, crumbled dry noodles (from Oriental noodle soup mix) or toasted sesame seeds, if desired.

4 servings

Prep time: 15 minutes

S E R V E   W I T H

RICE CAKES or BREAD

APRICOT FOSTER SUNDAES

1 can (17 ozs.) DEL MONTE Apricot Halves,
   undrained
⅓ cup firmly packed brown sugar
2 Tbsp. butter or margarine
1 pt. vanilla ice cream

Into small saucepan, drain apricot syrup. Bring to a boil. Reduce heat to low; simmer 4 minutes. Stir in sugar and butter; cook until thickened, stirring constantly. Add apricots; heat through. Spoon over scoops of ice cream. Garnish, if desired.

4 servings

Turn
back for
Cook Day
recipes

QUICK DAY

This yummy chicken salad is a cinch to make— no pots to clean, no waiting for the chicken to cool— since the chicken is cooked ahead on the Cook Day, page 19.

COOK DAY

This recipe could hardly be easier, but if extra chicken is baked with it, Country Chicken and Biscuits, page 24, is even simpler.

DO-AHEAD NOTE

■ Bake extra chicken.

CHICKEN PARMESAN NOODLE BAKE

1 pkg. (12 ozs.) extra wide
　noodles
8 half boneless chicken breasts,
　skinned (cook all and save
　4 for Quick Day, page 24)
½ tsp. rosemary, crushed

2 cans (14½ ozs. *each*) DEL
　MONTE® Italian Style
　Stewed Tomatoes
½ cup (2 ozs.) shredded
　mozzarella cheese
¼ cup (1 oz.) grated Parmesan
　cheese

1. Preheat oven to 450°F.

2. Cook noodles according to package directions; drain. Keep warm.

3. Meanwhile, sprinkle chicken with rosemary; season with salt and pepper, if desired. Arrange chicken in 13×9-inch baking dish. Bake, uncovered, 20 minutes or until chicken is no longer pink in center. Drain; remove chicken from dish. (Cool, cover and refrigerate 4 cooked chicken breasts for Quick Day, page 24.)

4. Drain tomatoes, reserving liquid. In large bowl, toss reserved liquid with noodles; place in baking dish. Top with chicken and tomatoes. Sprinkle with cheeses.

5. Bake 10 minutes or until heated through. Sprinkle with additional Parmesan cheese and garnish, if desired.　　　　*4 servings*

Prep & bake time: 35 minutes

S E R V E　　W I T H

CRISP GREEN SALAD
　6 cups chopped lettuce
　1 small red onion, sliced
　　Creamy Italian dressing

In large bowl, toss lettuce and
onion with dressing.
　　　　4 to 6 servings

CRUSTY FRENCH BREAD

23

Turn
page for
Quick Day
recipe

COUNTRY CHICKEN AND BISCUITS 🖵▨

**1 can (10¾ ozs.) condensed
cream of celery soup**
⅓ cup milk or water
4 half chicken breasts, cooked
and cut bite-size (cooked on
Cook Day, page 23)

**1 can (14½ ozs.) DEL MONTE®
Blue Lake Cut Green Beans,
drained**
**1 can (11 ozs.) refrigerated
biscuits**

1. Preheat oven to 375°F.

2. In large bowl, combine soup and milk. Gently stir in chicken and green beans; season with pepper, if desired. Spoon into 11×7-inch microwavable dish.

3. Cover with plastic wrap; slit to vent. Microwave on HIGH 8 to 10 minutes or until heated through, rotating dish once. If using conventional oven, cover with foil and bake at 375°F, 20 to 25 minutes or until hot.

4. Separate biscuit dough into individual biscuits. Immediately arrange biscuits over hot mixture. Bake in conventional oven about 15 minutes or until biscuits are golden brown and baked through.   *4 servings*

Prep & cook time: 30 minutes

SERVE WITH
**CHILLED DEL MONTE PINEAPPLE SLICES or
TOSSED GREEN SALAD**

Turn
back for
Cook Day
recipes

QUICK DAY

If you have a well-stocked pantry and keep cooked chicken in the freezer, you'll be able to toss this casserole together anytime.

If everyone wants pizza instead, use this chicken in place of turkey and make Rosemary Turkey Pizza, page 86.

Cook sausage and
extra chicken and
rice to make
Tomato Chicken
Gumbo, page 28,
later.

TIPS

■ To prebake sausage
and thighs, arrange in
large, shallow baking
pan. Place this pan,
uncovered, below pan of
tonight's Buffalo
Chicken Wings and bake
35 minutes or until
chicken is no longer
pink in center.

■ Marinade that has
come into contact with
raw meat must be boiled
for several minutes
before serving.

DO-AHEAD NOTE

■ Cook sausage and
extra chicken and rice.

HOT & SPICY BUFFALO CHICKEN WINGS

1 can (15 ozs.) DEL MONTE®
   Original Sloppy Joe Sauce
¼ cup hot salsa
1 Tbsp. vinegar, such as red wine
   or cider
20 chicken wings (about 4 lbs.)

6 chicken thighs (cook all and
   save for Quick Day, page 28)
½ lb. hot sausage links or Polish
   sausage (cook all and save for
   Quick Day, page 28)

1. Preheat oven to 400°F.

2. In small bowl, combine sloppy joe sauce, salsa and vinegar; cover and refrigerate ¼ of mixture to serve with cooked chicken wings. Set aside remaining sauce mixture to brush over chicken wings as they cook.

3. Arrange wings in single layer in large, shallow baking pan; brush both sides of wings with sauce mixture.

4. On middle rack in oven, bake chicken, uncovered, 35 minutes or until chicken is no longer pink in center, turning and brushing with remaining sauce mixture after 15 minutes. (Prebake sausage and thighs at same time, see Tips, page 26. Cool, cover and refrigerate all cooked sausage and thighs for Quick Day, page 28.) Serve wings with reserved ¼ cup sauce. Garnish, if desired.   *4 servings*

Prep time: 5 minutes
Bake time: 35 minutes

SERVE WITH

HOT BUTTERED RICE
2 cups uncooked long-grain white rice (cook all
   and save 1½ cups cooked rice for Quick
   Day, page 28)
1 Tbsp. butter or margarine
1 tsp. basil or thyme, crushed (optional)

Cook rice according to package directions. (Cool, cover and refrigerate 1½ cups cooked rice for Quick Day, page 28.) Toss remaining rice with butter and basil.

4 servings

TOSSED GREEN SALAD

27

Turn page for Quick Day recipe

TOMATO CHICKEN GUMBO

1 can (14 ozs.) chicken broth
½ lb. hot sausage links or Polish sausage, cooked and sliced (cooked on Cook Day, page 27)
1½ cups cooked white rice (cooked on Cook Day, page 27)
1 can (26 ozs.) DEL MONTE® Traditional or Chunky Garlic and Herb Spaghetti Sauce

6 chicken thighs, cooked, skinned, boned and cubed (cooked on Cook Day, page 27)
1 can (11 ozs.) DEL MONTE Summer Crisp Corn, drained
1 green bell pepper, diced

1. In 6-quart pot, bring broth and 2 cups water to a boil; add all remaining ingredients. Cover; cook over medium heat 10 minutes or until heated through.

2. Add additional water or broth for a thinner gumbo. For spicier gumbo, serve with hot red pepper sauce.

4 servings (about 2½ cups each)

Prep & cook time: 15 minutes

SERVE WITH

HOT BISCUITS or DINNER ROLLS

Turn back for Cook Day recipes

QUICK DAY

The chicken, sausage and rice are cooked on the Cook Day, page 27, to make this quick gumbo.

Or, if you're in the mood for something else, use these thighs (boned) and sausage to replace the beef in Beef Steak Chili, page 52. Just freeze this cooked rice for another day.

COOK DAY

While the pots are out, cook extra ravioli and sausage for another night's dinner—the reward is Ravioli Soup, page 32, in just minutes.

DO-AHEAD NOTE

■ Cook extra sausage and ravioli.

RAVIOLI WITH TOMATOES AND ZUCCHINI

3 pkgs. (9 ozs. *each*) fresh or
    frozen cheese ravioli or
    tortellini (cook all and save
    ⅓ for Quick Day, page 32)
1½ lbs. hot Italian sausage,
    crumbled (cook all and save
    half for Quick Day, page 32)

2 cans (14½ ozs. *each*) DEL
    MONTE® Diced Tomatoes
1 medium zucchini, thinly sliced
    and quartered
1 tsp. basil, crushed
½ cup ricotta cheese *or* 2 Tbsp.
    grated Parmesan cheese

1. In 8-quart pot, cook pasta according to package directions; drain. Keep hot. (Rinse one third of cooked pasta in cold water; cover and refrigerate for Quick Day, page 32.)

2. Meanwhile, in 6-quart pot, brown sausage over medium-high heat or until pink in center; drain. (Remove half of sausage from pot. Cool, cover and refrigerate for Quick Day, page 32.)

3. To remaining sausage in pot, add tomatoes, zucchini and basil. Cook, uncovered, over medium-high heat about 8 minutes or until zucchini is just tender-crisp, stirring occasionally. Season with pepper, if desired.

4. Spoon sauce over hot pasta. Top with ricotta cheese.   *4 servings*

Prep & cook time: 20 minutes

S E R V E   W I T H

ROMAINE AND BEET SALAD
  6 cups chopped romaine lettuce
  1 can (8¼ ozs.) DEL MONTE Sliced Beets,
    drained
  Blue cheese, crumbled
  Oil and vinegar dressing

In large bowl, toss lettuce,
beets and cheese with dressing.
4 to 6 servings

SESAME BREAD STICKS or FRENCH BREAD

Turn
page for
Quick Day
recipes

RAVIOLI SOUP

¾ lb. hot Italian sausage,
   crumbled and cooked (cooked
   on Cook Day, page 31)
**1 can (14½ ozs.) DEL MONTE®
   Italian Style Stewed Tomatoes**
1 can (14 ozs.) beef broth

1 pkg. (9 ozs.) fresh or frozen
   cheese ravioli or tortellini,
   cooked and drained (cooked
   on Cook Day, page 31)
**1 can (14½ ozs.) DEL MONTE
   Italian Green Beans, drained**
2 green onions, sliced

1. In 5-quart pot, combine sausage, tomatoes, broth and 1¾ cups water;
   bring to a boil over high heat.

2. Reduce heat to low; stir in ravioli, green beans and onions. Gently cook
   until ravioli are heated through. Season with pepper and sprinkle with
   grated Parmesan cheese, if desired.

4 servings (about 2½ cups each)

Prep & cook time: 15 minutes

S E R V E   W I T H

GARLIC BREAD
   ¼ **cup (½ stick) butter or margarine, softened**
   ⅛ **tsp. garlic powder**
   ½ **loaf French bread, sliced in half lengthwise**

In small bowl, combine butter
and garlic powder. Spread over
cut sides of French bread.
Bake at 450°F until lightly
browned, about 4 minutes.

4 servings

Turn
back for
Cook Day
recipes

QUICK DAY

Heating canned soups isn't much easier than preparing this hearty soup. The sausage and ravioli are cooked with a previous meal, page 31, for good fast food, now.

TIPS

■ Bake the bread while the soup cooks.
■ Spoon any leftover soup into a shallow bowl or dish for quick, safe cooling.

COOK DAY

When shaped into patties, this "meat loaf" bakes in about half the time. Bake extra patties to make Layered Noodle Bake, page 36, as a quick second meal.

DO-AHEAD NOTE

■ Cook extra patties and noodles.

ITALIAN MEAT LOAF PATTIES

2 pkgs. (12 ozs. e*ach*) extra wide noodles (cook all and save half for Quick Day, page 36)
1 Tbsp. butter or margarine, melted
1 can (15 ozs.) DEL MONTE® Italian or Original Sloppy Joe Sauce

2 lbs. ground beef or turkey (save half for Quick Day, see below)
1 cup dry bread crumbs
2 eggs, beaten
1 Tbsp. dried minced onions

1. Preheat oven to 375°F.

2. In 8-quart pot, cook noodles according to package directions; drain. (Rinse half of noodles in cold water; cover and refrigerate for Quick Day, page 36.) Toss remaining noodles with butter; keep hot.

3. Set aside half of sauce to brush on patties. In large bowl, combine remaining sauce with remaining ingredients; mix with fork. On large, greased baking sheet, shape meat mixture into 8 (1-inch-thick) oblong patties. Brush reserved sauce over patties.

4. Bake 20 minutes or until no longer pink in center. (Cool, cover and refrigerate half of cooked patties for Quick Day, page 36.) Serve remaining patties with hot, buttered noodles. Garnish, if desired.

4 servings

Prep time: 5 minutes   **Cook time:** 20 minutes

SERVE WITH

PEAS AND CORN

1 can (15¼ ozs.) DEL MONTE Whole Kernel Corn, drained
1 can (8½ ozs.) DEL MONTE Sweet Peas, drained
2 tsp. butter or margarine
¼ tsp. oregano, crushed
Dash cayenne pepper

In small saucepan, cook vegetables with butter, oregano and cayenne over medium heat until heated through, stirring occasionally. Garnish, if desired.

4 to 6 servings

35

Turn page for Quick Day recipes

LAYERED NOODLE BAKE

**1 can (26½ ozs.) DEL MONTE®
   Spaghetti Sauce with Green
   Peppers and Mushrooms**
**1 pkg. (12 ozs.) extra wide
   noodles, cooked (cooked on
   Cook Day, page 35)**

**4 Italian Meat Loaf Patties,
   cooked and cut bite-size
   (cooked on Cook Day,
   page 35)**
**1 pt. (16 ozs.) ricotta or cottage
   cheese**
**1 pkg. (8 ozs.) shredded
   mozzarella cheese**

1. Preheat oven to 350°F.

2. Onto bottom of shallow 3-quart or 13×9-inch baking pan, spread thin layer of sauce. Arrange half of noodles over sauce; cover with half of remaining sauce. Cover with meat, ricotta cheese and half of mozzarella cheese; top with layers of remaining noodles, sauce and mozzarella cheese.

3. Bake, uncovered, about 25 minutes or until heated through. Garnish, if desired.   *4 to 6 servings*

Prep time: 5 minutes
Bake time: 25 minutes

SERVE WITH

QUICK CAESAR SALAD
**6 cups torn romaine lettuce
   Croutons
   Bottled Caesar dressing**

In large bowl, toss lettuce and croutons with dressing. Sprinkle with grated Parmesan cheese, if desired.
4 to 6 servings

Turn
back for
Cook Day
recipes

Meat loaf patties
are transformed
into a delicious
lasagna-like dish
when layered with
lots of cheese,
spaghetti sauce
and noodles.

HEALTHY HINT

■ Substitute fat-free
ricotta cheese and
reduced-fat mozzarella
cheese.

TIPS

■ May be assembled
ahead.
■ Buy preshredded
mozzarella cheese.

COOK DAY

Use some of the
noodles tonight
while they're hot,
and save the rest
to make Tarragon
Tuna Pasta Salad,
page 40, later.

DO-AHEAD NOTE

■ Cook extra pasta.

CHEESEBURGER MACARONI

2 cups mostaccioli or elbow macaroni (cook all and save 3 cups for Quick Day, page 40)
1 lb. ground beef
1 onion, chopped

1 can (14½ ozs.) DEL MONTE® Original or Italian Style Stewed Tomatoes
¼ cup DEL MONTE Tomato Ketchup
1 cup (4 ozs.) shredded Cheddar cheese

1. Cook pasta according to package directions; drain. **(Rinse 3 cups cooked pasta in cold water; cover and refrigerate for Quick Day, page 40.)**

2. In large skillet, brown meat with onion; drain. Season with salt and pepper, if desired. Stir in tomatoes, ketchup and remaining pasta; heat through.

3. Top with cheese. Garnish with sliced green onions, if desired.

4 servings

Prep time: 8 minutes
Cook time: 15 minutes

SERVE WITH

BASIL CARROTS

1 can (14½ ozs.) DEL MONTE Sliced Carrots, drained
1 Tbsp. butter or margarine
½ tsp. basil, crushed

In small saucepan, heat carrots with butter and basil until heated through. Garnish, if desired. *4 servings*

PUDDING PARFAITS

4 DEL MONTE Pudding Cups, Vanilla
4 DEL MONTE Fruit Cups, Diced Peaches, drained
Non-dairy whipped topping
Crushed cookies

In tall glasses, layer pudding alternately with peaches and whipped topping. Sprinkle with cookies. Garnish, if desired. *4 servings*

Turn page for Quick Day recipes

TARRAGON TUNA PASTA SALAD

½ cup mayonnaise
½ tsp. tarragon or thyme, crushed
3 cups cooked, chilled mostaccioli
  or elbow macaroni (cooked
  on Cook Day, page 39)
2 stalks celery, sliced

1 can (6⅛ ozs.) solid white tuna in
  water, drained and broken
  into bite-size pieces
1 can (14½ ozs.) DEL MONTE®
  Peas and Carrots, drained

1. In large bowl, combine mayonnaise and tarragon. Add pasta, celery and tuna. Gently stir in peas and carrots.

2. Cover serving plates with lettuce, if desired. Top with salad. Garnish, if desired.   *4 servings*

Prep time: 8 minutes

S E R V E   W I T H

CREAM OF TOMATO SOUP

BREAD STICKS or CRACKERS

PINEAPPLE GLAZED CHEESECAKE

1 can (8 ozs.) DEL MONTE Crushed Pineapple,
  undrained
⅓ cup apricot jam or preserves
1 small (8-inch) cheesecake

Drain pineapple, reserving 2 tablespoons liquid. In small bowl, combine reserved liquid and jam. Spoon pineapple over cheesecake; drizzle with jam mixture.   *6 servings*

Turn
back for
Cook Day
recipes

QUICK DAY

Tarragon is a nice complement to the peas, carrots and tuna in this quick salad. Precooked pasta from the Cook Day, page 39, make this salad extra convenient.

HEALTHY HINT

■ Use light mayonnaise instead of regular mayonnaise.

TIP

■ Can be made ahead.

COOK DAY

Cooked over hot coals or under the broiler, these kabobs are delicious! Save half of the grilled meat for the Quick Day, page 44.

TIP

■ To prevent burning of wooden skewers, soak skewers in water for 10 minutes before assembling kabobs.

DO-AHEAD NOTE

■ Cook extra steak and rice.

BEEF KABOBS WITH APRICOT GLAZE

2 lbs. sirloin steak (cook all and save half for Quick Day, page 44)

1 can (17 ozs.) DEL MONTE® Apricot Halves, undrained

1 Tbsp. cornstarch

1 tsp. Dijon mustard

½ tsp. basil, crushed

1 small green bell pepper, cut into ¾-inch pieces

4 medium mushrooms, cut in half

4 to 8 skewers

1. Cut meat into 2 equal portions. Cut 1 portion into 1½-inch cubes; set aside remaining portion.

2. Drain apricot syrup into small saucepan. Blend in cornstarch until dissolved. Cook over medium heat, stirring constantly, until thickened. Stir in mustard and basil. Set aside.

3. Thread meat cubes, apricots, green pepper and mushrooms alternately onto skewers; brush with apricot mixture before and during cooking. Grill kabobs and reserved 1-pound piece of meat over hot coals (or broil) about 5 minutes per side or to desired doneness. **(Cool, cover and refrigerate extra piece of cooked meat for Quick Day, page 44.)** Garnish, if desired. *4 servings*

Prep time: 10 minutes
Cook time: 15 minutes

SERVE WITH

HOT COOKED RICE

1¼ cups uncooked long-grain white rice (cook all and save 1 cup cooked rice for Quick Day, page 44)

1 Tbsp. butter or margarine

Cook rice according to package directions. **(Cool, cover and refrigerate 1 cup cooked rice for Quick Day, page 44.)** Toss remaining rice with butter. *4 servings*

Turn page for Quick Day recipes

STROGANOFF STUFFED POTATOES 🔲

4 medium baking potatoes
1 onion, chopped
6 medium mushrooms, sliced
1 Tbsp. butter or margarine
1 lb. grilled sirloin steak, cut bite-
size (cooked on Cook Day,
page 43)

1 can (14½ ozs.) DEL MONTE®
Mixed Vegetables, drained
1 cup sour cream

1. Pierce each potato with fork; place on paper towel in microwave oven. Microwave on HIGH about 16 minutes or until tender, rotating once.

2. Meanwhile, in large skillet on stovetop, cook onion and mushrooms in butter until tender. Add meat and vegetables; heat through. Remove from heat; stir in sour cream.

3. Split tops of potatoes; fluff insides with fork. Season with salt and pepper, if desired. Spoon meat mixture over potatoes.   *4 servings*

Prep time: 5 minutes
Cook time: 16 minutes

S E R V E   W I T H

EASY RICE PUDDING
1 cup cooked rice (cooked on Cook Day,
page 43)
4 DEL MONTE Pudding Cups, Vanilla
Ground nutmeg

In medium bowl, combine rice and pudding. Sprinkle with nutmeg. Garnish, if desired.
4 servings

Turn
back for
Cook Day
recipes

QUICK DAY

This stuffed potato is a meal in itself. It's especially quick since it uses meat grilled on Cook Day, page 43.

Or, make Grilled Chicken Taco Salad, page 12, using this beef instead of chicken.

HEALTHY HINT

■ Use light or nonfat sour cream; use a nonstick skillet and reduce butter.

COOK DAY

While preparing tonight's beef stir-fry, place half of the steak in a marinade and refrigerate for another night's dinner, page 48.

TIPS

■ Partially freeze the meat for easier slicing.

■ After extra rice is cooked, cover loosely and refrigerate. Or, rice may be frozen for several months in a tightly sealed freezer bag.

DO-AHEAD NOTES

■ Marinate flank steak.

■ Cook extra rice.

STIR-FRY TOMATO BEEF

2 cups uncooked long-grain white rice (cook all and save half for Quick Day, page 48)

2 lbs. flank steak (cook 1 lb. and marinate remaining 1 lb. for Quick Day, page 48)

1 Tbsp. cornstarch

1 Tbsp. soy sauce

2 cloves garlic, minced

1 tsp. minced ginger root *or* ¼ tsp. ground ginger

1 Tbsp. vegetable oil

1 can (14½ ozs.) DEL MONTE® Original Style Stewed Tomatoes

1. Cook rice according to package directions. (Cool, cover and refrigerate half of cooked rice for Quick Day, page 48.) Keep remaining rice hot.

2. Cut meat crosswise into 2 equal pieces, about 1 pound each. (Cover and marinate 1 pound of meat in refrigerator overnight for Quick Day, see step 1 on page 48.) Cut remaining meat in half lengthwise, and then cut crosswise into thin slices.

3. In medium bowl, combine cornstarch, soy sauce, garlic and ginger. Add sliced meat; toss to coat.

4. Preheat oil in large skillet over high heat. Add meat; cook, stirring constantly, until browned. Add tomatoes; cook until thickened, about 5 minutes, stirring frequently.

5. Serve over hot rice. Garnish with chopped cilantro or green onions, if desired. *4 to 6 servings*

Prep time: 10 minutes
Cook time: 15 minutes

S E R V E   W I T H

TOSSED GREEN SALAD

47

Turn page for Quick Day recipes

MARINATED FLANK STEAK WITH PINEAPPLE

1 can (15¼ ozs.) DEL MONTE®
Pineapple Slices In Its Own
Juice, undrained
¼ cup teriyaki sauce

2 Tbsp. honey
1 lb. flank steak (saved and
marinated on Cook Day,
page 47)

1. (If meat was marinated on Cook Day, go to step 2.) For marinade, drain pineapple, reserving 2 tablespoons juice. Set pineapple aside. In shallow 2-quart dish, combine reserved juice, teriyaki sauce and honey; mix well. Add meat; turn to coat. Cover and refrigerate at least 30 minutes or overnight. Remove meat from marinade, reserving marinade.

2. Grill meat over hot coals (or broil), brushing occasionally with marinade. Cook about 4 minutes on each side for rare; about 5 minutes on each side for medium; or 6 minutes on each side for well done. During last 4 minutes of cooking, brush pineapple slices with marinade; grill until heated through.

3. Slice meat across grain; serve with pineapple. Garnish, if desired.

4 servings

Prep & marinate time: 35 minutes   **Cook time:** 10 minutes

S E R V E   W I T H

SESAME RICE
   3 cups cooked long-grain white rice (cooked on Cook Day, page 47)
2 green onions, sliced
2 Tbsp. toasted sesame seeds

In 1½-quart microwavable dish, toss rice, 2 teaspoons water, onions and sesame seeds. Cover; microwave on HIGH 2 to 3 minutes.   *4 servings*

HONEY MUSTARD CARROTS
1 Tbsp. honey
1 tsp. Dijon mustard
1 jar (16 ozs.) DEL MONTE Cut Carrots, drained

In 1-quart microwavable dish, combine honey and mustard. Add carrots; toss to coat. Cover; microwave on HIGH 2 to 3 minutes.   *4 servings*

Turn back for Cook Day recipe

QUICK DAY

Nothing is tastier than meat that marinates overnight!

TIPS

■ Sprinkle cold rice with a teaspoon of water, then cover tightly with vented plastic wrap before reheating in the microwave.

■ Marinade that has come into contact with raw meat must be boiled several minutes before serving.

■ Start the coals about 40 minutes before you plan to cook.

COOK DAY

For another meal, cook an extra pound of steak to make Beef Steak Chili, page 52.

DO-AHEAD NOTE

■ Cook extra steak.

GRILLED STEAK

2½ lbs. beef steak, such as flank, sirloin or round steak (cook all and save 1 lb. for Quick Day, page 52)

Garlic salt
Pepper

1. Season meat with garlic salt and pepper. Grill over hot coals (or broil) about 5 minutes on each side or until desired doneness is reached.

2. Cut meat diagonally across grain into thin slices. (Cool, cover and refrigerate 1 pound cooked meat for Quick Day, page 52.)

4 servings

Prep & cook time: 10 minutes

S E R V E   W I T H

SPINACH SALAD WITH PEARS AND RED ONIONS

6 cups torn spinach leaves
1 can (16 ozs.) DEL MONTE® Sliced Pears, drained
½ red onion, thinly sliced
Oil and vinegar dressing

In large bowl, toss spinach, pears and onion with dressing.
4 to 6 servings

BAKED POTATOES WITH SOUR CREAM AND CHIVES

51

Turn page for Quick Day recipes

BEEF STEAK CHILI

2 cans (14½ ozs. *each*) DEL MONTE® Chili Style Chunky Tomatoes

1 can (15 ozs.) black or kidney beans, rinsed and drained

1 lb. grilled beef steak slices, diced (cooked on Cook Day, page 51)

1 can (8¾ ozs.) DEL MONTE Whole Kernel Corn, drained

2 Tbsp. fresh lime juice

1. In large skillet, cook tomatoes and beans over medium-high heat 5 minutes or until slightly thickened, stirring occasionally.

2. Stir in meat, corn and lime juice; heat through. Season with salt and pepper, if desired.

3. Sprinkle with chopped cilantro, if desired.

4 servings

Prep & cook time: 15 minutes

S E R V E   W I T H

PINEAPPLE SPRITZER
   Ice
   DEL MONTE Pineapple Juice, chilled
   Sparkling water

For each serving, fill tall glass with ice. Fill with ¾ juice and ¼ water.

CORN BREAD or FRENCH BREAD

Turn back for Cook Day recipes

QUICK DAY

For easy chili making, plan to toss an extra steak on the grill a day or two ahead.

Rather have salad? Make Mandarin Chicken Salad, page 20, using this cooked steak instead of chicken.

TIP

■ For a spicier chili, add chili powder, cayenne pepper or hot pepper sauce.

COOK DAY

This recipe makes a double batch of meat sauce. Serve some tonight and freeze the rest for later.

TIPS

■ If you don't have an 8-quart pot, cook the pasta in two batches.
■ To freeze sauce, cool sauce slightly in an uncovered freezer container, then tightly seal and freeze up to 6 months.

DO-AHEAD NOTES

■ Cook extra pasta.
■ Cook extra sauce to freeze.

ZUCCHINI MEAT SAUCE WITH PASTA

2 pkgs. (12 ozs. *each***) shell
macaroni or corkscrew pasta
(cook all and save half for
Quick Day, page 56)**
2 lbs. ground beef
2 onions, chopped

2 cans (26½ ozs. *each***) DEL
MONTE® Spaghetti Sauce
With Garlic**
**1 can (14½ ozs.) DEL MONTE
Diced Tomatoes, undrained**
2 small zucchini, thinly sliced

1. In 8-quart pot, cook pasta according to package directions; drain.
(Rinse half of pasta in cold water; cover and refrigerate for Quick
Day, page 56.) Keep remaining pasta hot.

2. In 6-quart pot, brown meat over medium-high heat. Season with salt and
pepper, if desired; drain. Add onions; cook until tender. Stir in spaghetti
sauce and tomatoes; cook 5 minutes, stirring occasionally. (Pour half of
sauce into freezer container; cool, cover and freeze for another meal.)

3. Add zucchini to remaining sauce; cover and cook over medium heat
7 to 10 minutes or until zucchini is tender. Serve sauce over hot pasta.
Sprinkle with grated Parmesan cheese and garnish, if desired.

4 servings

Prep & cook time: 30 minutes

S E R V E   W I T H

TOSSED GREEN SALAD

HERBED or PLAIN FRENCH BREAD

Turn
page for
Quick Day
recipes

CAESAR SHRIMP PASTA SALAD

1 can (14½ ozs.) DEL MONTE®
Pasta Style Chunky
Tomatoes, undrained
1 lb. cooked tiny shrimp
6 cups cooked shell macaroni or
corkscrew pasta (cooked on
Cook Day, page 55)

1 small cucumber, diced
1 cup Caesar dressing
3 green onions, sliced

1. Drain tomatoes, reserving ⅓ cup liquid. In large bowl, combine reserved liquid with tomatoes and remaining ingredients. Season with salt and pepper, if desired.

2. Cover and refrigerate until serving time. Garnish, if desired.

4 servings (2½ cups each)

Prep time: 10 minutes

S E R V E   W I T H

CREAMY ASPARAGUS POTATO SOUP

1 can (15 ozs.) DEL MONTE Asparagus
Spears, drained
1 can (14½ ozs.) DEL MONTE New Potatoes,
drained
½ tsp. thyme, crushed
⅛ tsp. garlic powder
1 can (14 ozs.) chicken broth
1 cup milk or half & half

1. Place asparagus, potatoes, thyme and garlic powder in food processor or blender (in batches if needed); process until smooth.

2. Pour into medium saucepan; add broth. Bring to a boil. Stir in milk; heat through. (*Do not boil.*) Season with salt and pepper, if desired. Serve hot or cold. Thin with additional milk or water, if desired. *4 servings*

CRUSTY FRENCH BREAD

Turn
back for
Cook Day
recipe

QUICK DAY

An extra batch of pasta gets cooked ahead on the Cook Day, page 55, so this salad can be ready in minutes.

COOK DAY

This dinner is tasty and quick. Country Skillet Hash, page 60, will be every bit as good, but even easier since you cook the meat for it tonight.

TIP

■ Look for the economical "family pack" pork chops offered at some meat counters. You often save by buying the larger quantity.

DO-AHEAD NOTE

■ Cook extra pork chops.

LOUISIANA PORK CHOPS

2 tsp. garlic powder
½ tsp. *each* black pepper, white pepper and cayenne
8 pork chops (¾ inch thick) (cook all and save 4 for Quick Day, page 60)

2 Tbsp. butter or margarine
1 can (14½ ozs.) DEL MONTE® Cajun or Original Style Stewed Tomatoes

1. In small bowl, combine garlic powder and peppers; rub onto both sides of meat. In large skillet, heat butter over medium-high heat. Add meat; cook 5 minutes on each side. Drain. (Cool, cover and refrigerate 4 cooked chops for Quick Day, page 60.)

2. Add tomatoes to skillet; reduce heat to medium. Cover; cook until meat is no longer pink in center, about 10 minutes. Remove meat to serving dish; keep warm.

3. In same skillet, continue cooking tomatoes over medium-high heat until thickened, stirring occasionally; spoon over meat. *4 servings*

Prep time: 5 minutes   **Cook time:** 20 minutes

S E R V E   W I T H

CORN NUGGET CORNBREAD STUFFING

Cornbread stuffing mix (see package for additional required ingredients)
1 can (15¼ ozs.) DEL MONTE Whole Kernel Corn, drained

Prepare 4 servings stuffing according to package directions. Add corn; toss. Heat according to package directions for stuffing mix.
4 servings

BROILED PINEAPPLE RINGS

1 can (15¼ ozs.) DEL MONTE Pineapple Slices In Its Own Juice, drained
Brown sugar
Ground cinnamon

Arrange pineapple slices on broiler pan; sprinkle with sugar and cinnamon. Broil until golden brown, about 30 seconds. *4 servings*

TOSSED GREEN SALAD

59

Turn page for Quick Day recipes

COUNTRY SKILLET HASH

1 medium onion, chopped
2 cloves garlic, minced
2 Tbsp. butter or margarine
1 can (14½ ozs.) DEL MONTE®
    Whole New Potatoes, drained
    and diced
1 can (14½ ozs.) DEL MONTE
    Original Style Stewed
    Tomatoes

4 pork chops (¾ inch thick),
    cooked and diced (cooked on
    Cook Day, page 59)
1 green bell pepper, chopped
½ tsp. thyme, crushed

1. In large skillet, cook onion and garlic in butter over medium heat until tender; add potatoes, tomatoes, meat, green pepper and thyme. Cook 5 minutes, stirring frequently.

2. Season with salt and black pepper, if desired.   *4 servings*

Prep time: 5 minutes
Cook time: 15 minutes

S E R V E   W I T H

HOT BISCUITS

DESSERT JEWELS
  2 DEL MONTE Gel Snack Cups, cut into cubes
    (any flavor)
  1 can (17 ozs.) DEL MONTE Fruit Cocktail,
    drained

In medium bowl, toss gel with fruit.   *4 servings*

Turn
back for
Cook Day
recipes

QUICK DAY

As quick as it is tasty, this hash is made from already cooked pork chops, page 59. Stewed tomatoes give this dish a new twist.

This pork may be used in place of turkey to make Skillet Turkey Chili, page 87.

TIP

■ The hash may be topped with a poached or fried egg.

COOK DAY

Thick juicy pork chops smothered in a tasty Italian sauce—who could resist? Save some of these chops to make Pork Fried Rice, page 64.

TIP

■ When extra meat and rice stop steaming, cover loosely and refrigerate.

DO-AHEAD NOTE

■ Cook extra pork chops and rice.

ITALIAN PORK CHOPS

4 cups uncooked long-grain white rice (cook all and save 7 to 8 cups cooked rice for Quick Day, page 64)

8 large pork chops (½ inch thick) (cook all and save 4 for Quick Day, page 64)

1 tsp. basil, crushed

1 can (26 ozs.) DEL MONTE® Spaghetti Sauce with Mushrooms or Chunky Italian Herb Spaghetti Sauce

1 green bell pepper, cut into thin strips

1. Cook rice according to package directions. (Cool, cover and refrigerate 7 to 8 cups cooked rice for Quick Day, page 64.) Keep remaining rice hot.

2. Preheat broiler. Sprinkle meat with basil; season with salt and black pepper, if desired. Place meat on broiler pan. Broil 4 inches from heat about 6 minutes on each side or until no longer pink in center. (Cool, cover and refrigerate 4 chops for Quick Day, page 64.) Keep remaining chops warm.

3. In 11×7-inch microwavable dish, combine sauce and green pepper. Cover with plastic wrap; slit to vent. Microwave on HIGH 5 to 6 minutes or until green pepper is tender-crisp and sauce is heated through. Add meat; cover with sauce. Microwave 1 minute. Serve over hot rice.   *4 servings*

Prep & cook time: 25 minutes

S E R V E   W I T H

SAVORY MIXED VEGETABLES

1 can (14½ ozs.) DEL MONTE Mixed Vegetables, drained

2 tsp. butter or margarine

¼ tsp. oregano, crushed Dash garlic powder

In small saucepan, cook vegetables with butter, oregano and garlic powder over medium heat until heated through, stirring occasionally.

4 servings

63

Turn page for Quick Day recipes

PORK FRIED RICE

1 onion, finely chopped
2 Tbsp. vegetable oil
7 to 8 cups cooked rice (about
　　2½ cups uncooked rice)
　　(cooked on Cook Day,
　　page 63)
4 cooked pork chops, diced
　　(cooked on Cook Day,
　　page 63)

1 can (14½ ozs.) DEL MONTE®
　　Peas and Carrots, drained
3 green onions, sliced
3 to 4 Tbsp. soy sauce

1. In large skillet or wok, cook chopped onion in hot oil until tender-crisp.

2. Add cooked rice; cook over medium heat 8 minutes or until heated through, stirring frequently.

3. Stir in meat, vegetables and soy sauce; heat through. Season with pepper, if desired. *4 servings*

Prep & cook time: 15 minutes

S E R V E   W I T H

SPINACH PINEAPPLE SALAD

6 cups torn spinach leaves
1 can (8 ozs.) DEL MONTE Pineapple Tidbits
　　In Its Own Juice, drained
Oil and vinegar dressing

In large bowl, toss spinach and pineapple with dressing.
4 to 6 servings

FORTUNE COOKIES

Turn
back for
Cook Day
recipes

QUICK DAY

Fried rice is a dish almost everyone loves. This version makes an especially easy weeknight supper, since the meat and rice are cooked ahead on the Cook Day, page 63.

Or, this pork could be used instead of chicken to make Mandarin Chicken Salad on page 20.

COOK DAY

This light meal will fill you up but not out. Plan to do the Quick Day menu, page 68, the day after this menu is cooked, so the fish is at its best.

DO-AHEAD NOTE

■ Cook extra fish.

SNAPPY HALIBUT SKILLET

½ tsp. thyme, crushed
2 lbs. halibut or other firm white
   fish (cook all and save ½ lb.
   for Quick Day, page 68)
1 Tbsp. olive oil
1 onion, chopped

1 clove garlic, minced
1 Tbsp. cornstarch
1 can (14½ ozs.) DEL MONTE®
   Stewed Tomatoes, No Salt
   Added
¼ cup sliced green onions

1. Sprinkle thyme over both sides of fish. In large skillet, cook fish in hot oil over medium-high heat until fish flakes easily when tested with fork. (Cool, cover and refrigerate about ½ pound fish for Quick Day, page 68.) Remove remaining fish to plate; keep warm.

2. In same skillet, cook chopped onion and garlic until tender. Stir cornstarch into tomatoes; pour into skillet. Cook, stirring frequently, until thickened. Return fish to skillet; top with green onions. Heat through.   *4 servings*

Prep time: 5 minutes
Cook time: 10 minutes

S E R V E   W I T H

BUTTERED GREEN BEANS

FRENCH BREAD

ANGEL FOOD CAKE WITH FRUIT

4 slices angel food cake
1 can (16 ozs.) DEL MONTE Lite Chunky
   Mixed Fruit, chilled and drained
6 ozs. vanilla yogurt

Top each cake slice with fruit
and yogurt. Garnish, if
desired.   *4 servings*

67

Turn
page for
Quick Day
recipes

FISHERMAN'S SOUP

1 onion, chopped
1 clove garlic, crushed
1 Tbsp. vegetable oil
3 Tbsp. flour
2 cans (14 ozs. *each*) low-salt chicken broth
1 can (15¼ ozs.) DEL MONTE® Whole Kernel Corn, No Salt Added, undrained

1 can (14½ ozs.) DEL MONTE Whole New Potatoes, drained and chopped
½ lb. cooked halibut (cooked on Cook Day, page 67)

1. In large saucepan, cook onion and garlic in hot oil over medium heat until onion is tender. Stir in flour; cook 1 minute. Stir in broth; cook until thickened, stirring occasionally. Stir in corn and potatoes.

2. Discard skin and bones from fish; cut fish into bite-size pieces.

3. Just before serving, add fish to soup; heat through. Stir in chopped parsley or sliced green onions, if desired.   *4 to 6 servings*

Prep time: 5 minutes
Cook time: 10 minutes

S E R V E   W I T H

HOT CRUSTY FRENCH ROLLS

FRUIT 'N' YOGURT

1 can (16 ozs.) DEL MONTE Fruit Naturals (any fruit), chilled and drained
1 pt. (16 oz.) low-fat vanilla yogurt

In medium bowl, combine fruit with yogurt.   *4 servings*

Turn back for Cook Day recipes

QUICK DAY

This delicious soup takes advantage of already cooked fish, page 67.

Or, use this fish in place of tuna in the Tarragon Tuna Pasta Salad, page 40.

HOLIDAYS MADE EASY

There's no way around it—cooking the holiday dinner takes a little extra time. But with good planning, even the family chef can enjoy the festivities. Here's a menu that is mapped out for you, dividing most of the preparation steps over three evenings. You do a little every night—just what you can manage at the end of a busy day. Again, the ingredient listing on each recipe is a convenient shopping list. Don't forget to add the dinner rolls, cranberry sauce and all the makings for your favorite mashed or sweet potatoes.

On the day of the holiday be sure to involve everyone with the last-minute preparations. This way, the holiday feast goes more smoothly and it's fun for everyone—even the cook.

HOLIDAY MENU

Sparkling Holiday Cheer with Fruited Ice (page 77)

■

Shrimp & Chili Sauce over Cream Cheese (page 78)
Pickle & Vegetable Platter (page 78)*

■

Zesty Green Salad (page 79)
Savory Green Bean Bake (page 79)*
Golden Corn Pudding (page 80)*

■

Mashed potatoes or sweet potatoes (recipes not included)

■

Roasted Turkey & Herb Bread Stuffing (pages 81 and 82)*
Easy Old-Fashioned Gravy (page 83)*
Cranberry sauce (purchased)
Assorted dinner rolls (purchased)

■

Chocolate Pear Tart (page 84)*
Creamy Fruit Bavarian (page 85)*

*photographed on opposite page

8 ozs. linguine or spaghetti,
uncooked
1 lb. ground beef, ground turkey
or mild Italian sausage
3 cups coarsely chopped onions
(cover and refrigerate 2 cups
for Herb Bread Stuffing,
page 81)
1 clove garlic, minced

2 cans (14½ ozs. *each*) DEL
MONTE® Pasta Style Chunky
Tomatoes, undrained
1 can (8 ozs.) DEL MONTE
Tomato Sauce
About ¼ cup (1 oz.) grated
Parmesan cheese
1 loaf (1 lb.) French bread (save
¼ of loaf to make croutons,
page 79)

1. Cook pasta according to package directions; drain and keep hot.

2. In large skillet, brown meat with 1 cup onions and garlic; drain.

3. Add tomatoes and tomato sauce. Cook, stirring frequently, 15 minutes.

4. Spoon sauce over hot pasta; sprinkle with cheese. Serve with bread.

4 servings

Prep time: 10 minutes
Cook time: 20 minutes

S E R V E   W I T H

**TOSSED SALAD WITH HERB TOMATO
DRESSING**
½ cup Herb Tomato Dressing (page 73)
4 cups torn lettuce
¼ cup sliced green onions

1. Prepare Herb Tomato
Dressing. Reserve ½ cup
dressing for this salad. (Cover
and refrigerate remaining
Herb Tomato Dressing for
Zesty Green Salad, page 79.)

2. Place lettuce and onions in
salad bowl. Toss with reserved
½ cup dressing.

HERB TOMATO DRESSING
- **1 can (14½ ozs.) DEL MONTE® Diced Tomatoes, undrained**
- **¼ cup red wine vinegar**
- **1 Tbsp. Dijon mustard**
- **1 Tbsp. honey**
- **½ tsp. basil, crushed**
- **½ cup olive oil**

1. Drain tomatoes reserving liquid. Pour liquid into medium bowl; blend in vinegar, mustard, honey and basil.

2. Stir in tomatoes and oil.

3. Refrigerate until ready to use.   *About 2⅓ cups*

Prep time: 15 minutes

D O - A H E A D H O L I D A Y C O O K I N G	Page #	Prep Time
Cut extra onions for Herb Bread Stuffing while chopping them for Pasta Pronto.	81	5 minutes
Refrigerate the rest of Herb Tomato Dressing for Zesty Green Salad.	79	2 minutes
Make croutons for Zesty Green Salad.	79	5 minutes (20 mins. cook)
If frozen, place turkey in refrigerator to thaw.	82	2 minutes
Chill juices for Sparkling Holiday Cheer.	77	3 minutes
Make Fruited Ice for Sparkling Holiday Cheer.	77	1½ hours (to freeze)
Get out the holiday serving dishes.		10 minutes

SWEET & SOUR PORK CHOPS AND RICE
PRE-HOLIDAY COOK DAY 2

1 cup uncooked long-grain white rice

1 can (8 ozs.) DEL MONTE® Pineapple Chunks In Its Own Juice, undrained

2 Tbsp. vegetable oil

8 pork chops, trimmed (cook all and save 4 for Pre-Holiday Cook Day 3, page 75)

1 green bell pepper, chopped

¾ cup sweet and sour sauce

1. Cook rice according to package directions.

2. Drain pineapple, reserving ¼ cup juice.

3. Heat oil in large skillet over medium-high heat. Season meat with salt and pepper, if desired. Add meat to skillet; cook until browned on both sides and no longer pink in center; drain. (Cool, cover and refrigerate 4 pork chops for Pre-Holiday Cook Day 3, page 75.) Keep remaining meat warm.

4. Pour reserved pineapple juice into skillet. Add pineapple, green pepper and sweet and sour sauce. Cover; cook over medium heat, 5 minutes. Add meat; heat through. Serve over hot cooked rice. *4 servings*

Prep time: 5 minutes
Cook time: 30 minutes

DO-AHEAD HOLIDAY COOKING	Page #	Prep Time
Cut vegetables for the Pickle & Vegetable Platter; place in cold water and refrigerate.	78	20 minutes
Toast almonds for both Savory Green Bean Bake topping and Chocolate Pear Tart crust.	79, 84	5 minutes
Slice celery and chop parsley for Herb Bread Stuffing.	81	10 minutes
Prepare and bake Chocolate Pear Tart crust.	84	15 minutes (bake 8 min.)
Prepare and refrigerate the Creamy Fruit Bavarian, but leave out the gel.	85	10 minutes

FESTIVE PORK SALAD PRE-HOLIDAY COOK DAY 3

1 can (14½ ozs.) DEL MONTE®
 Mexican Style Stewed
 Tomatoes, cut up
1 pkg. (1¼ ozs.) taco seasoning
 mix
4 cooked pork chops, cut into
 thin strips (cooked on Pre-
 Holiday Cook Day 2, page 74)
1 can (8¾ ozs.) DEL MONTE
 Whole Kernel Corn, drained

2 large heads romaine lettuce
 (wash both and refrigerate
 1 head for Zesty Green
 Salad, page 79)
1 cup (4 ozs.) shredded Cheddar
 cheese
 Tortilla chips, coarsely broken

1. In large skillet, cook tomatoes with taco seasoning until thickened, about 5 minutes. Add meat and corn; toss to coat.

2. Place lettuce in salad bowl; top with meat mixture.

3. Sprinkle with cheese and tortilla chips. Garnish with sour cream and sliced green onions, if desired. Serve with hot buttered flour tortillas, if desired.   *4 to 6 servings*

Prep time: 10 minutes
Cook time: 5 minutes

DO-AHEAD HOLIDAY COOKING	Page #	Prep Time
Cook and refrigerate giblets for Easy Old-Fashioned Gravy.	83	5 minutes (cook 1½ hours)
Assemble and refrigerate Savory Green Bean Bake, but do not put on topping.	79	5 minutes
Wash, dry and wrap 1 head romaine lettuce in paper towels. Refrigerate in sealed plastic bag for Zesty Green Salad.	79	10 minutes
Prepare Herb Bread Stuffing; cover and refrigerate.	81	5 minutes (cook 15 min.)
Finish preparing Chocolate Pear Tart; cover and refrigerate.	84	10 minutes

THE HOLIDAY COUNTDOWN

4 hours before serving time	Stuff and roast the turkey, pages 81 and 82. Set the table.
3 hours before serving time	Gently stir the gel cubes into the Creamy Fruit Bavarian, page 85. Chill until dessert time.
	Make the Golden Corn Pudding, page 80, but don't bake it; cover and refrigerate. (Remember to get it out of the refrigerator at least 30 minutes before baking.)
	Tear or chop the romaine lettuce for Zesty Green Salad, page 79. Refrigerate it in plastic food storage container or large plastic food storage bag.
	Arrange the Pickle & Vegetable Platter, page 78; cover and refrigerate.
1½ hours before serving time	Pour the Sparkling Holiday Cheer, page 77, into the punch bowl. (Do not add ginger ale and Fruited Ice at this time; add these when ready to serve.)
	Make your favorite mashed or sweet potato recipe, if desired.
When guests arrive	Prepare Shrimp & Chili Sauce over Cream Cheese, page 78.
	Add ginger ale and Fruited Ice to Sparkling Holiday Cheer.
	Serve appetizers and beverages.
40 minutes to go	Put the Golden Corn Pudding, page 80, and any extra stuffing in the oven when the turkey comes out.
	Sprinkle topping over Savory Green Bean Bake, page 79, and bake.
30 minutes to go	Make Easy Old-Fashioned Gravy, page 83. Reduce heat to low; keep warm until ready to serve, stirring occasionally.
20 minutes to go	Carve the turkey and arrange it on a platter with the Herb Bread Stuffing.
	Place potatoes in oven to keep warm until serving time. (Or, microwave a few minutes before serving.)

continued

10 minutes to go	Toss Zesty Green Salad, page 79, with Herb Tomato Dressing, page 73.
	Pop the dinner rolls in the oven for a couple of minutes.
	Place all the food in serving dishes and arrange on the table. (Don't forget serving utensils for each!) Check the menu to be sure everything is out.
After Dinner	Refrigerate all leftovers within 1 hour of dinner. Remove stuffing from turkey cavities and refrigerate separately. Freeze any turkey, stuffing and gravy that won't be used within 2 or 3 days.

ICE BREAKERS
SPARKLING HOLIDAY CHEER WITH FRUITED ICE

1 can (17 ozs.) DEL MONTE®
   Chunky Mixed Fruit,
   undrained

1 can (46 fl. ozs.) DEL MONTE
   Pineapple Juice, chilled
1 qt. cranberry juice, chilled
1 qt. ginger ale, chilled

1. Into 6-cup ring mold, pour undrained fruit. Freeze about 1½ hours or until fruit is set. Add water until ½ inch from top of mold. Freeze overnight or until frozen solid.

2. Pour juices into punch bowl. Just before serving, add ginger ale.

3. Dip ice ring into warm water to unmold. Float in punch bowl.

About 28 (½-cup) servings

Prep time: 10 minutes   **Freeze time:** 1½ hours

T I P
To make your holiday affair more relaxing, have the appetizers ready to serve before the guests arrive. This way, you'll have time for last minute meal preparation.

SHRIMP & CHILI SAUCE OVER CREAM CHEESE

1 pkg. (8 ozs.) cream cheese or
   Neufchâtel cheese, softened
   Lettuce leaves (optional)
½ cup DEL MONTE® Chili Sauce
   or Seafood Cocktail Sauce

¼ lb. cooked tiny shrimp
   Assorted crackers

1. Place cream cheese on plate over lettuce leaves, if desired.

2. Just before serving, spoon sauce and shrimp over cream cheese. Serve with crackers.
6 to 8 servings

Prep time: 5 minutes

T I P

For a festive touch, shape the cheese into a log, ball or oval and then roll it in finely chopped parsley.

PICKLE & VEGETABLE PLATTER

1 jar (12 ozs.) DEL MONTE Tiny
   Kosher Dill Pickles or Dill
   Pickle Chips, drained
1 jar (12 ozs.) DEL MONTE
   Sweet Midget Pickles,
   drained
1 jar (11¾ ozs.) DEL MONTE
   Hot Chile Peppers, drained

1 can (7 ozs.) green or ripe olives
   drained
Crisp vegetables: green onions,
   mushrooms, carrot sticks,
   green or red bell pepper
   strips, celery sticks or
   radishes (cut on Pre-Holiday
   Cook Day 2, page 74)

Arrange all ingredients on serving platter.
6 to 8 servings

Prep time: 20 minutes

THE MAIN EVENT
ZESTY GREEN SALAD

6 cups torn or chopped romaine
lettuce (saved from Pre-
Holiday Cook Day 3, page 75)
Herb Tomato Dressing (saved
from Pre-Holiday Cook
Day 1, page 73)

Croutons (bread saved from
Pre-Holiday Cook Day 1,
page 72, see Tip below)

1. In salad bowl, place lettuce; toss with dressing.

2. Top with croutons. Season with salt and pepper, if desired.

6 to 8 servings

Prep time: 5 minutes

T I P

To make croutons, cut French bread into ¾-inch cubes; place in a shallow baking pan. Drizzle with olive oil or melted butter and toss. Bake at 350°F for 20 minutes or until golden and crisp. Store in a tightly sealed container.

SAVORY GREEN BEAN BAKE

2 cans (14½ ozs. *each*) DEL
MONTE® Blue Lake Cut
Green Beans, drained
1 can (10¾ ozs.) condensed cream
of mushroom soup

1 can (2.8 ozs.) French fried
onions
¼ cup chopped toasted almonds
(toasted on Pre-Holiday Cook
Day 2, page 74)

1. In medium bowl, toss green beans with soup and half of onions. Spoon into 1½-quart casserole.

2. Combine remaining onions with almonds; set aside for topping.

3. Bake at 350°F 30 minutes or until hot and bubbly. Top with almond mixture; bake 5 minutes.

6 to 8 servings

Prep time: 5 minutes   **Bake time:** 35 minutes

GOLDEN CORN PUDDING

2 Tbsp. butter
3 Tbsp. flour
1 can (14¾ ozs.) DEL MONTE®
Cream Style Golden Sweet
Corn
¼ cup yellow cornmeal

2 eggs, separated
1 pkg. (3 ozs.) cream cheese,
softened
1 can (8¾ ozs.) DEL MONTE
Whole Kernel Corn, drained

1. Preheat oven to 350°F.

2. In medium saucepan, melt butter. Add flour; stir until smooth. Blend in cream style corn and cornmeal. Bring to a boil, stirring constantly, over medium heat.

3. Place egg yolks in small bowl; stir in ½ cup hot corn mixture. Pour mixture back into saucepan. Add cream cheese and whole kernel corn.

4. Place egg whites in narrow bowl; beat until stiff peaks form. With rubber spatula, gently fold egg whites into corn mixture.

5. Pour into ungreased 1½-quart straight-sided baking dish. Bake 30 to 35 minutes or until lightly browned. Garnish, if desired.

4 to 6 servings

Prep time: 10 minutes
Bake time: 35 minutes

T I P
You can assemble this pudding up to 3 hours ahead, if you keep it refrigerated. Remove it from the refrigerator about 30 minutes before baking.

HERB BREAD STUFFING

2 cups chopped onions (cut on Pre-Holiday Cook Day 1, page 72)
4 stalks celery, sliced (cut on Pre-Holiday Cook Day 2, page 74)
½ cup butter or margarine
1½ tsp. poultry seasoning

1½ cups chicken broth
2 pkgs. (8 ozs. *each*) herb bread stuffing
½ cup chopped parsley (cut on Pre-Holiday Cook Day 2, page 74)

1. In large skillet, cook onions and celery in butter until tender.

2. Add seasoning and broth; simmer 10 minutes.

3. Place stuffing and parsley in large bowl; toss with onion mixture. (This slightly dry consistency is desired for stuffing that is to be baked inside the turkey.) *About 10 cups*

Prep & cook time: 20 minutes

T I P S

Bake any extra stuffing in a covered baking dish. First add a little extra chicken broth, so it's nice and moist but not soggy. Cover and bake at 350°F for about 30 minutes or until hot.

For safety, stuff the turkey just before roasting it, never ahead of time. Always remove all of the stuffing from the turkey as soon as possible after removing it from the oven.

ROASTED TURKEY & HERB BREAD STUFFING

1 (8- to 12-lb.) fresh or frozen, thawed turkey, rinsed and dried inside and out (save the giblets for Easy Old-Fashioned Gravy, page 83)

1 recipe Herb Bread Stuffing (page 81)
½ cup butter or margarine, softened

1. Preheat oven to 325°F. Season turkey cavities with salt and pepper, if desired. Just before roasting, spoon stuffing into both cavities. (*Do not pack stuffing.*) Fasten cavity closed with metal skewers or sew closed with string. Bend wing tips under body, tucking under skin of neck to secure. Tie drumsticks together with string.

2. Rub turkey with butter. Season with salt and pepper, if desired. Place turkey, breast side up, on rack in large roasting pan. Insert meat thermometer into the thickest part of the thigh, avoiding the bone.

3. Roast turkey 2½ to 4 hours (see Tips below) or until internal temperature reaches 180° to 185°F, basting every hour. Remove from oven and let stand about 20 minutes before carving. (Reserve drippings and scrapings in pan for preparing Easy Old-Fashioned Gravy, page 83.) Garnish, if desired.

10 to 12 servings

Prep time: 15 minutes   **Roast/Stand time:** 2½ to 4½ hours

T I P S

A stuffed turkey bakes about 20 minutes for every pound at 325°F. The turkey is done when the juices run clear when turkey is pierced or when the drumsticks move up and down easily.

Plan to have the turkey ready about 30 minutes before dinnertime to allow standing time as well as time to make the gravy before carving the turkey.

For easier cleanup and shorter cooking time, use an oven cooking bag. (Be sure to follow the package directions.)

Be sure to add cranberry sauce, dinner rolls and the makings for mashed or sweet potatoes to your shopping list.

EASY OLD-FASHIONED GRAVY

Drippings & browned scrapings
(saved from Roasted Turkey
pan, page 82)

Chopped, cooked turkey giblets
(saved from Roasted Turkey,
page 82, see Tips below)

⅓ cup flour
1¾ cups turkey giblet broth (liquid
that giblets are cooked in, see
Tips below)

1. Pour drippings and scrapings into 2-cup glass measuring cup. Let stand until it separates, about 5 minutes.

2. Slowly pour off and discard top translucent liquid from drippings until only 1½ cups of liquid and browned scrapings remain.

3. In large saucepan, stir flour with the remaining 1½ cups drippings until smooth; cook over low heat until it starts to thicken.

4. Slowly stir in broth; cook until thickened and smooth. (If gravy becomes lumpy, strain.)

5. Add giblets; heat through. Season with salt and pepper, if desired.

About 3 cups

Prep time: 8 minutes
Cook time: 5 minutes

T I P S

Cook turkey giblets in broth or water for about 1½ hours or until giblets are tender. Refrigerate giblets and cooking liquid until it's time to make Easy Old-Fashioned Gravy.

For an even simpler gravy, replace the giblet cooking broth with 1 can of chicken broth.

For a darker gravy, use a little bottled browning sauce.

THE LAST ACT
CHOCOLATE PEAR TART

1 cup chocolate cookie crumbs
½ cup chopped toasted almonds
  (toasted on Pre-Holiday Cook
  Day 2, page 74)
¼ cup sugar
⅓ cup butter or margarine, melted
1 pkg. (6 ozs.) semi-sweet
  chocolate chips

1 tsp. instant coffee crystals
1 can (16 ozs.) DEL MONTE®
  Bartlett Pear Halves,
  undrained
1 tsp. unflavored gelatin
1 cup whipping cream, whipped to
  stiff peaks

1. Preheat oven to 350°F.

2. In medium bowl, combine cookie crumbs, almonds and sugar. Stir in butter. Pat onto bottom and 1 inch up sides of 9-inch removable-bottom tart or pie pan. Bake 8 minutes; cool.

3. In food processor or blender, combine chocolate and coffee; process until well blended.

4. Drain pears, reserving ½ cup syrup in small saucepan. Cover and refrigerate pears. Sprinkle gelatin over reserved syrup. Let stand 5 minutes. Bring to a boil. Add syrup mixture to chocolate in food processor; process until chocolate melts. Scrape chocolate mixture into medium bowl; fold in whipped cream.

5. Spoon filling into crust. Chill at least 4 hours or until set.

6. Just before serving, partially cut each pear half lengthwise into ¼-inch-thick slices, starting ½ inch from point of pear, leaving pointed end intact. Arrange pears over tart, fanning pears. Garnish with additional cookie crumbs and chopped almonds, if desired.   *8 to 10 servings*

Prep time: 35 minutes   **Bake time:** 8 minutes   **Chill time:** 4 hours

T I P

To toast almonds, spread almonds in a shallow baking pan. Bake at 350°F, stirring occasionally, until crisp and golden brown, 10 to 15 minutes. For easier cutting, chop almonds while still warm.

CREAMY FRUIT BAVARIAN

1 pkg. (3 ozs.) cream cheese,
   softened
¼ cup sugar
1 can (17 ozs.) DEL MONTE®
   Fruit Cocktail, drained
1 can (8 ozs.) DEL MONTE
   Pineapple Tidbits In Its Own
   Juice, drained

1 cup (4 ozs.) thawed frozen non-
   dairy whipped topping
2 DEL MONTE Gel Snack Cups,
   Strawberry Flavored

1. In medium bowl, blend cream cheese with sugar. Stir in fruit. Gently fold in whipped topping.

2. Cut gel into cubes; gently fold into cream cheese mixture. Cover and chill several hours. Garnish with additional gel cubes, if desired.

4 to 6 servings

Prep time: 10 minutes

SECRETS TO QUICK CLEAN-UP

✔ Tidy up as you go, putting away cooking ingredients and loading things into the dishwasher as you use them. Wipe up all spills immediately.

✔ Partially fill pans that have food burned on in hot water with a tablespoon of dishwasher detergent or baking soda. Soak utensils covered with sugary or starchy foods, like rice (and eggs, too), in cold water. Fill greasy pans with hot, soapy water. Use oven cleaner to clean the BBQ grill in minutes.

✔ Re-use measuring cups and spoons by first measuring dry ingredients and then liquids and fats.

✔ Use a 1-quart glass measure for measuring, mixing and cooking in the microwave. Use heavy or nonstick skillets and pans for stovetop cooking. Choose pans roomy enough to prevent spills or boil-overs. Line baking and broiler pans with foil and use roasting bags when appropriate.

✔ Never reheat foods in a pan that has baked-on food around its edges.

✔ Air dry dishes. (It's more sanitary and a lot less work.)

ROSEMARY TURKEY PIZZA
POST-HOLIDAY QUICK DAY 1

1 can (14½ ozs.) DEL MONTE®
   Italian Style Stewed Tomatoes
1½ cups bite-size cooked turkey
   (Roasted Turkey, page 82)
½ tsp. rosemary, crushed
1 (12-inch) prepared prebaked
   pizza crust

2 cups (8 ozs.) shredded
   mozzarella cheese, divided
1 green, yellow or red bell pepper,
   sliced
⅓ cup sliced green onions

1. Preheat oven to 450°F.

2. Drain tomatoes, reserving liquid. In medium skillet, combine reserved liquid with turkey and rosemary. Cook 5 minutes or until liquid evaporates.

3. Place crust on baking sheet. Chop tomatoes; spread evenly over crust. Cover with half of cheese; top with turkey mixture, pepper slices and green onions. Sprinkle with remaining 1 cup cheese.

4. Bake 10 minutes or until cheese is hot and bubbly. *4 to 6 servings*

Prep time: 10 minutes
Bake time: 10 minutes

T I P
Refrigerated pizza dough is every bit as good as your favorite pizzeria's. For best results, be sure to follow the package directions.

S E R V E   W I T H
RAW VEGETABLES (FROM HOLIDAY DINNER) or TOSSED GREEN SALAD

SKILLET TURKEY CHILI
POST-HOLIDAY QUICK DAY 2

2 slices bacon, cut into ½-inch
    pieces
1 large onion, chopped
2 cloves garlic, crushed
2 cups bite-size cooked turkey
    (Roasted Turkey, page 82)

1 to 2 tsp. chili powder
1 can (14½ ozs.) DEL MONTE®
    Mexican Style Stewed
    Tomatoes
1 can (15 ozs.) kidney or black
    beans, drained

1. In large skillet, cook bacon over medium heat until just crisp; remove and set aside. Drain skillet.

2. Add onion and garlic to skillet; cook and stir until tender. Add turkey and chili powder; cook 5 minutes, stirring occasionally.

3. Add tomatoes. Bring to a boil. Stir in reserved bacon and beans. Reduce heat; simmer 5 minutes.   *4 servings*

Prep time: 5 minutes
Cook time: 15 minutes

S E R V E   W I T H

TOSSED GREEN SALAD

DINNER ROLLS (FROM HOLIDAY DINNER)

CHOCOLATE PEARS WITH ICE CREAM
  1 pt. (16 oz.) vanilla ice cream
  1 can (16 ozs.) DEL MONTE Sliced Bartlett
    Pears, drained
  Chocolate sauce or ice cream topping

Spoon ice cream into bowls.
Top with pears; drizzle with
chocolate sauce.
4 to 6 servings

8 WAYS TO CUT FAT

Look over the recipe to identify foods that contribute fat, like egg yolks, cheese, meats and, of course, oils and butter. Once identified, here's what you do.

1. Replace some of the oil in salad dressings with Del Monte fruit juices, stewed tomato liquid or water. Or, choose from the many reduced-fat dressings on the market.

2. Instead of heavy gravies, serve salsas with meat, fish and poultry.

3. When cooking, decrease or eliminate the amount of oil used with nonstick skillets and/or vegetable oil cooking spray.

4. Remove poultry skin after roasting, but before marinating or sautéing. Trim the fat off meats. Buy less fatty cuts, like round steak, rather than fattier cuts, like chuck. Keep meat portions reasonable–4 ounces (uncooked) meat per person is ample.

5. Use egg whites to replace all or part of the yolks; for example, use 2 whole eggs and 2 egg whites instead of 4 whole eggs. Or, try egg substitutes.

6. Use hard, robust cheeses, such as Parmesan, and strong cheeses, like blue, so a little is all you need. Use nonfat and low-fat cheeses, milk, cream cheese and sour cream.

7. When you use oil or butter, use as little as possible.

8. Eat meatless meals several times a week.

HELPFUL KITCHEN HINTS

When it comes to saving foods safely for later use, it is better to be cautious rather than casual. These general guidelines should help you make wise decisions about storing and handling foods.

GOOD HABITS HELP

✔ Start with clean hands, utensils, surfaces, dish towels and sponges.

✔ Handle food as little as possible with your hands, choosing instead to mix with clean utensils.

✔ Wash your hands and cutting surfaces with hot, soapy water after handling raw meats, fish and poultry, and especially before handling any foods that will not be cooked.

✔ Marinate foods, covered, in the refrigerator.

✔ Keep hot foods hot (140°F or above), and cold foods cold (40°F or below).

✔ Never re-freeze foods that have thawed.

✔ The more ideal the storage and handling conditions, the fresher the foods stay. Keep the refrigerator at 40°F and the freezer at 0°F. Pantry temperatures should be 65°F or cooler.

✔ Buy cold foods last at the store and get them home and refrigerated immediately.

STORING AND USING SAVED FOODS

✔ As soon as cooked foods stop steaming, and at least within 2 hours of cooking, cover and refrigerate them in small portions in shallow containers (less than 2 inches deep). Or, freeze them within 2 hours of cooking, wrapped tightly in foil or sealed tightly in plastic freezer bags or containers.

✔ Label and date food for storage. Throw food out if you have any question about its safety.

✔ Bone large cooked meats; remove stuffing from meats and poultry; divide large quantities of food into smaller portions before freezing or refrigerating.

✔ Don't crowd food either in the refrigerator or freezer since air needs to circulate. Frequently wash the refrigerator and freezer walls and shelves with warm, soapy water and toss out old food.

✔ Thaw foods in the refrigerator overnight or in the microwave as directed on the package. Foods thawed in the microwave must be cooked as soon as thawed. Use foods thawed in the refrigerator within a day after thawing.

✔ Bring leftover soups and stews to a full boil and other leftovers to 165°F before serving again.

FACTS ABOUT CANNED PRODUCTS

✔ Ideally, canned foods should be stored in a dry place, at 65°F or cooler.

✔ Transfer contents of opened cans of vegetables, fruits or tomatoes into a clean plastic or glass container with a tight-fitting lid. Remember that Del Monte canned products do not contain preservatives and once opened should be refrigerated and used within a few days. Once opened, foods in jars, such as pickles, ketchup and mustard, need to be tightly sealed and refrigerated.

✔ Do not use cans that are bulging, leaking or extremely dented.

✔ Even though properly stored canned foods will maintain their peak quality for years, you should rotate your canned goods so you use your most recent purchases last.

TIPS FOR FAST FOOD

Our 2 NITE RECIPES™ are designed to help you get dinner on the table quickly. The recipes are simple, the ingredients are readily available and the number of pots and pans used is kept to a minimum. Here are our tips for fast food.

1. Keep a well-stocked pantry, refrigerator and freezer.

2. Take your shopping list to the store, so you get just what you need and don't forget anything. Buy convenience products—preseasoned canned tomatoes, preshredded cheeses, prebaked pizza crusts and prewashed lettuce.

3. Read each recipe completely before starting. Start with the longest cooking recipe first. Don't wait around while the water boils or a dish simmers; use every spare minute to prep the next dish, load the dishwasher or clean up.

4. Rinse out bowls and pans to re-use them for several steps in a recipe. (Dishes containing raw meats, fish, poultry or eggs must be washed in hot, soapy water before re-use.)

5. Ask someone else to set the table and get the dinner beverages out.

TO FREEZE OR NOT TO FREEZE

Many foods freeze well, as long as they are well sealed in heavy foil, plastic freezer bags or containers. To prepare meals in a hurry, freeze a variety of items you use frequently to create your own convenience products.

✔ Foods that freeze well include: grated and shredded cheeses, flour tortillas, cooked rice and pasta, chopped fresh herbs, grated ginger, raw and cooked meat and poultry, butter, buttermilk, cooked soups, stews and sauces (not cream based).

✔ Foods that do not freeze well include: raw eggs, mayonnaise, milk, potatoes and vegetables with a high water content, such as celery.

✔ Do not re-freeze seafood, meats or poultry that have been previously frozen, unless you cook them first. Check package labels or ask the butcher to see if a product is fresh or has been previously frozen.

✔ Put foods in the freezer as soon as possible after purchase or after cooking, and avoid keeping foods several days in the refrigerator before freezing.

Who to call for answers to food storage questions:
U.S. Department of Agriculture Meat and Poultry Hotline
1-800-535-4555 10:00 a.m. to 4:00 p.m. Eastern time
Monday through Friday.

This table tells you approximately how long cooked and uncooked foods may be stored, refrigerated and frozen.

ITEM	RAW		COOKED	
	Refrigerated (40°F)	Frozen (0°F)	Refrigerated (40°F)	Frozen (0°F)
Fish	1 day	3 to 6 mos.	1 day	2 to 3 mos.
Poultry	1 to 2 days	9 to 12 mos.	3 to 4 days	4 to 6 mos.
Beef, Pork & Lamb	3 to 5 days	4 to 9 mos.	3 to 4 days	2 to 3 mos.
Meat & Poultry in broth, sauce or gravy			1 to 2 days	2 to 3 mos.
Ground Meat & Poultry	1 to 2 days	3 to 4 mos.	1 to 2 days	1 to 2 mos.
Ham Slices			3 to 4 days	1 to 2 mos.
Sausage	1 to 2 days	1 to 2 mos.	1 to 2 days	1 to 2 mos.
Smoked Sausage			7 days	3 to 4 mos.
Eggs In Carton	3 weeks	Don't freeze		
Separated		Don't freeze	1 day	12 mos.
Hard-Cooked		Don't freeze	7 days	Don't freeze
Soups & Stews			3 to 4 days	2 to 3 mos.
Rice & Pasta (shelf stable)	indefinitely	indefinitely	3 to 4 days	1 to 2 mos.
Cheese: Hard & Semi-Hard	1 to 4 weeks	6 to 8 weeks		
Soft Ripened Cheese, Uncreamed Cottage Cheese, Cream Cheese	3 to 14 days	4 to 8 weeks		
Butter (salted)	1 to 2 mos.	6 to 9 mos.		
Heavy Cream	1 week from date on carton	3 to 6 mos.		
Tortillas, Baked Bread	1 week	2 weeks		
Fresh Herbs	3 to 14 days	1 to 2 mos. (chopped)		

Reference: USDA Booklet, "Preventing Foodborne Illness"

INDEX

METRIC CONVERSION CHART

VOLUME MEASUREMENTS (dry)

1/8 teaspoon = 0.5 mL

1/4 teaspoon = 1 mL

1/2 teaspoon = 2 mL

3/4 teaspoon = 4 mL

1 teaspoon = 5 mL

1 tablespoon = 15 mL

2 tablespoons = 30 mL

1/4 cup = 60 mL

1/3 cup = 75 mL

1/2 cup = 125 mL

2/3 cup = 150 mL

1/4 cup = 175 mL

1 cup = 250 mL

2 cups = 1 pint = 500 mL

3 cups = 750 mL

4 cups = 1 quart = 1 L

VOLUME MEASUREMENTS (fluid)

1 fluid ounce (2 tablespoons) = 30 mL

4 fluid ounces (1/2 cup) = 125 mL

8 fluid ounces (1 cup) = 250 mL

12 fluid ounces (1 1/2 cups) = 375 mL

16 fluid ounces (2 cups) = 500 mL

WEIGHTS (mass)

1/2 ounce = 15 g

1 ounce = 30 g

3 ounces = 90 g

4 ounces = 120 g

8 ounces = 225 g

10 ounces = 285 g

12 ounces = 360 g

16 ounces = 1 pound = 450 g

DIMENSIONS

1/16 inch = 2 mm

1/8 inch = 3 mm

1/4 inch = 6 mm

1/2 inch = 1.5 cm

3/4 inch = 2 cm

1 inch = 2.5 cm

OVEN TEMPERATURES

250°F = 120°C

275°F = 140°C

300°F = 150°C

325°F = 160°C

350°F = 180°C

375°F = 190°C

400°F = 200°C

425°F = 220°C

450°F = 230°C

BAKING PAN SIZES

Utensil	Size in Inches/ Quarts	Metric Volume	Size in Centimeters
Baking or Cake Pan (square or rectangular)	8×8×2	2 L	20×20×5
	9×9×2	2.5 L	22×22×5
	12×8×2	3 L	30×20×5
	13×9×2	3.5 L	33×23×5
Loaf Pan	8×4×3	1.5 L	20×10×7
	9×5×3	2 L	23×13×7
Round Layer Cake Pan	8×1½	1.2 L	20×4
	9×1½	1.5 L	23×4
Pie Plate	8×1¼	750 mL	20×3
	9×1¼	1 L	23×3
Baking Dish or Casserole	1 quart	1 L	—
	1½ quart	1.5 L	—
	2 quart	2 L	—